A Biographical Reflection of Being a Latin American Clinical Social Worker in the United States

A Biographical Reflection of Being a Latin American Clinical Social Worker in the United States

César M. Garcés Carranza, Ph.D.

Ordering Information:

For orders and inquiries, please contact:
1-888-404-1388
www.goldtouchpress.com
book.orders@goldtouchpress.com

Printed in the United States of America

Para

Sofía y Vivian

Acknowledgment

To my clients/patients, for they are the ones who have grown me and cured me. They have curiously enough shown me the road less traveled, for without them I would not know the things I know now.

Thank you!

César M. Garcés Carranza, Ph.D.

CONTENTS

My Story

SEPTEMBER-2020

Summary:

In this book, the author describes the actual context of clinical /psychiatric social work in the United States, also the principal areas of the professional practice and the needed education and credentials required to practice this profession. Later, will highlight his identity as a Latin American. The main points of this personal exploration rest in a reflection that pretends to explain the advantages of being a Latin American clinical/psychiatric social worker in the United States, finally, recommendations and suggestions will be made for the Latin American clinical social work movement that has been growing up for the last few years.

As a way of invitation, the author believes that social workers should contribute in initiatives of research, not only to demonstrate their effectiveness in their therapeutic interventions, but also to promote the recognition and acceptance of other colleagues in the field of health and mental health. Clinical social workers should understand that they play an important role identifying and treating a series of psychosocial problems, which encompass from the post-traumatic stress to the emotional reactions that people suffer when they face problems that are related to their mental health. As a profession that is based on human rights, the specialty of clinical social work has an essential function in all societies, facilitating the communities to raise their voice and defend their rights along with others. The power of clinical social work rest in its own professional foundation, which implies its capacity to create a participatory democracy, to link communities in sustainable futures and protecting human rights.

Key Words:

Social work, clinical social work, psychiatric social work, mental health, community mental health clinicals

I.

Areas of Clinical Social Work Practice and Required Credentials

For the past 35 years this author has been practicing as a clinical/psychiatric social worker both in the hospital setting and in community outpatient mental health settings in New York City and on Long Island, with people from different social, ethnic and multicultural backgrounds, especially with the Latin American communities. As a clinical social worker, he can identify the major psychosocial and emotional problems, including crisis interventions, providing counseling, and exploring alternatives to identify and apply alternatives to face emotional problems such as depression and anxiety. Restoring the functioning throughout implementation of a plan of action and providing adequate interventions to people with severe stress conditions is part of his daily practice in mental health settings. The focus of his interventions is the basis of his concentration of what happens in *"the here and now"* and not in the past.

Mental health, as part of the overall health of people, is a component of human growth and therefore of the development of nations. Mental health is not only based on subjective conditions; it is also based on objective conditions. A comprehensive look at this statement assumes an understanding of mental health as an element that is inserted in the society. Mental health is related to the deployment of different human capacities in different moments of life, the things that we do, be them small or big. It involves building and developing active links that are reality transformers, that allows us to take care of our personal needs and psychic wellbeing, as well as of others.

Social work is a profession and academic discipline that is committed to improve the social and emotional wellbeing of people, changes, and social justice. This profession works towards research and practice to improve the quality of life of people, groups, and the community where they live. Social work develops interventions through research, administration, local community organizations, direct practice, prevention, and education. Often, research is focused in areas such as human development, public administration, evaluation of programs and community development. Social workers are organized in local professional, national, and international groups. Social work is an interdisciplinary field that includes theories of economics, education, sociology, medicine, psychology, philosophy, and anthropology (NASW, 2012).

To talk about mental health among Latinos in the United States, is also to talk about poverty and inequality. The present situation of health and mental health is an important indicator of the actual conditions of most of the Latino population. This offers us a different look of living in poverty, exclusion, and inequality that our communities go through should be taking care as a key component of a comprehensive strategy against poverty and mental problems.

Cultural Concepts:

The author's daily activities with clients/patients and families who only speak Spanish in a country where the dominant language is English, shows an understanding about the complexity of the hospital emergency room which is the entrance to the hospital. These experiences can also be extended to patients and families of countries of different languages. Those social workers who do not have knowledge of the Spanish language, often have difficulty communicating with clients/patients and their families. The author's experience in the hospital setting is extensive. He has worked at the Bronx Lebanon Hospital Center, Bronx, New York for over two decades (1989-2013), and by being admitted to a hospital when he first arrived in the United States and did not speak English. He was interviewed by doctors and nurses who did not speak Spanish, and with the help from a translator who neither spoke well his language. As a result of this, he almost got killed because the translator did not understand what he said and gave wrong information to the doctor who was examining him. Therefore, he very well understands the problems that clients/patients face when they are interviewed by people who do not speak their language. According to Campinha-Bacote (1998), cultural competence is about cultural knowledge, attitudes, behavior and including politics that train professionals to be able to function in different intercultural contexts.

As the United States changes into a more diverse racial, multicultural, and ethnical country, as social workers we need to understand the different ethnical perspectives, cultural and values of people to whom we provide our professional services. Lack of knowledge and the understanding of social and cultural differences could end up in negative consequences for people from different cultural and ethnic backgrounds. An adequate intervention is required for social workers to respect and not to judge people who need our professional intervention.

This implies respect for the beliefs about health and mental health problems, as well as the solution of a problem that is presented by the client/patient. Cultural competence in this area of intervention requires general knowledge of assistance actions that are common in society, the institutions involved are culturally separated, which could be difficult for an adequate intervention, or could be that the services being offered are culturally inadequate or they are not available. The administrators of hospitals and community mental health centers should develop strategies to hired, retain, and promote within these institutions, teams of diverse multicultural professionals that are competent in the areas where they provide professional services. By doing so, clients/patients could efficiently communicate in their language.

To build hospitals and competent community mental health centers, means changing perceptions about other cultures or ethnic groups. How do they communicate and operate? This means that the structure, leadership, and activities of an organization should reflect the values, perspectives, lifestyle, and people's priorities. Because social changes are happening fast, organizations are beginning to understand the need to hire professionals who are culturally and ethnically competent. As social workers, we are becoming aware that, if we do not improve our professional skills, we will be paralyzed as a professional organization.

The present hostile political climate of the United States could cause fear, anxiety, depression, and toxic stress among the Latino population. Intimidation, bullying and hostility in the schools could also cause stress among Latino students. The salary discrepancy along with the use of social networks and their complexity of how they impact the mental health is also an important factor. According to some experts of mental health, stress is not the only principal cause of emotional problems, but it can also contribute to exacerbate the need for people with these conditions to take care of their mental health. Even though clinical social workers treat these types of emotional problems, Latinos, as a group, have less probability of access to mental health services, especially children and elderly adults.

The modern clinical social worker must adapt to the world globalization where institutions are having an impact on the rules and unilateral practices. The progressive increase of social culturally different consumers, especially in hospitals and community mental health centers, constitute a challenge for clinical social workers. The National Association of Social Workers (NASW, 2016), defines social work as "a profession that promotes social changes, solutions to human relationships and empowers people to improve their social wellbeing." By utilizing theories of human behavior and social systems, social workers intervene in places where people relate to their social environment. The principles and human rights are fundamentals for clinical social work.

The assertion of a group of social work representatives around the world clearly asserted that the elements that encompasses the modern practice of this profession are interrelated within the outside world and the internal psychological experiences of the individual. To better understand how to be able to help under these circumstances, clinical social workers must develop the ability to assess and intervene in different places with individuals, families, and with groups of people from different ethnic and cultural groups. Such interventions must be understood within the legal functional context and needs of services for the consumers, with the firm foundation against racism and discrimination. The borders between countries are diminishing because of economic pressures, geopolitics, regions, wars, internal and ethnic conflicts that promote among other things, migrations. That is why cultural competency in clinical social work is a need and expectation of all public services that reflects the multicultural increase in a diverse society, country or region where we live (Walker, S., & Beckett, C., 2005).

Certain types of connotative languages could be ambivalent, causing misunderstandings that could scare the client/patient, as well as the family. Because of this, the clinical social worker and family members could end up in conflictive situations. There is a need for the communication to be clear and adequate between the clinical social worker and the client/patient/family. Language obstacles could be overcome when the clinical social worker speaks the same language of the client/patient and family members. Communication is not easy, even when people have the same history of experiences and shared values or speak the same language. There are situations where couples have been living together for more than thirty years and still have misunderstandings. It is no surprise, therefore, to find lack of communication among people who do not know each other. Whatever is said could be heard in a different way by the other person or it also could be misunderstood.

Lumb, D. (1999), defines cultural competence as "the group of knowledge and skills that the social worker and other health care professionals have to be able to be competent multicultural with clients." Clinical social work deals with different components of culture, which include gender, race, sexual orientation, religion, etc. Green, J. (1999), author of *"Cultural Awareness in the Human Services,"* was certain when he said that the practice of cultural competence must have knowledge base, professional training and proper interventions to be able to understand people of different cultures and ethnic backgrounds. Betancourt, J. R (2001), also mentioned that culture is a group of learned beliefs, shared values, styles of living and communication, practice, costumes, and points of view on what has to do with functions and social relationships.

Based on the author's extensive professional experience as a clinical social worker (1985-present) with people from different Latin American countries and other parts of the world, not everybody who speaks Spanish are the same. On the contrary, these people have different social histories, values, cultural and religious costumes. The countries of Spanish speaking population are geographically different. They have specific costumes as well as ethnic and cultural blends. The people from Latin America are associated with nineteen countries of Spanish speaking language, in the Caribbean, Central and South America. Brazil is the exception, where the official language is Portuguese, and Guyana where the official language is English, and Suriname where the official language is Dutch.

When the clinical social worker is from a country different than the ethnic group of the client/patient, misunderstandings are common. The social worker who lacks knowledge of the language of the client/patient must be careful and avoid making false assumptions about the expectations of the treatment that will be offered. The clinical social worker and the client/patient bring their own social and cultural patterns to the experience of the interview, which must be immediately solved, to be able to get equal access and quality of treatment services.

Cultural Competence Obstacles:

Even though language is important, this is not the only obstacle. Obstacles can be any aspect of attention of health care that contributes to the wrong use of it. Obstacles can affect the quality of services that are offered and can also contribute to racial and ethnic Disparities. These include:

1. Lack of diversity in the health care center.
2. A health care center that is inadequately designed to fulfil the needs of a diverse population of clients/patients.
3. Communication problems among health care providers and clients/patients of different ethnic groups, culture, language, social and religions.

Cultural competence is one of the principle ingredients for the elimination of disparities in hospitals and in community mental health care centers. For that reason, when clinical social workers speak of psychosocial and mental health problems without understanding cultural differences that are brought during the interaction with the clients/patients, these can be intensified. Simply said, those hospitals and community mental health centers that respect and respond to the sociocultural and linguistics of a diverse population, can have positive results on the provision of health and mental health care services. For the development of cultural competence, it is required to examine preferences and prejudices, searching for models to follow and to share as much as possible with other people who have the passion for cultural competence. The term cultural competence came from the publication in Mental Health by the psychologist Paul Pedersen in 1998, at least a decade before the term cultural competence became popular.

According to Coon, D. (2000), most definitions of cultural competence are shared with a diversity of professionals that are from the mental health field. According to Carter, R. (1999), some of the benefits of developing cultural competence in any organization, are:

1. Increases respect and mutual understanding among those involved.
2. Increases creativity to solve problems through new perspectives, ideas, and strategies.
3. Decreases unwanted surprises that could delay progress in the intervention.
4. Increases trust and cooperation from the client/ patient.
5. Increases participation and collaboration with other multicultural groups.
6. Helps to overcome fear of making mistakes, to competence or conflict. For example. by understanding and accepting people from different cultures, there is more. probabilities that these people will feel comfortable.
7. Promote the inclusion and equality of rights.

Statistical Data of Latinos in the United States:

In 2005, the Latino population was the largest minority group in the United states, consisting of: 14% of the total population, compared with 13% of African Americans and 5% of Asians. By 2059, it is expected that the Latinos will be almost 29% of the population. According to the US Census Bureau (2006) and the Pew Hispanic Center (2015), more than double than the representation for 2005. New York State is the home of more than 3.1 million Latinos or 16%

of the population (Pew Hispanic Center, 2015). Latinos of Caribbean descendants is the largest group of people from Latin America (58%), followed by those of Latin American descendants (15%), follow by (12%) of Mexican descendants and (9%) of Central America.

According to the Pew Hispanic Center Report (2015), Latinos are 25% of the total population of New York State; 38% are White, 23% are African Americans and 14% are from Asia and the Pacific Islands. Most Latinos live in East Harlem, New York, in "El Barrio" as it is referred by the Latino residents. According to the 2000 US Census, Latinos were 52.1% of the population of East Harlem, New York, followed by 35% African Americans, Whites 7.7%. Among Latinos, Puerto Ricans is the largest group in East Harlem or 57.75% of the population, followed by 16.9% of Mexicans, and 7.7% from the Dominican Republic. According to the Pew Hispanic Center (2015), the Latino population has grown 14% or 2'485,260. According to the New York Controller's Office (2016), almost one in every five people in identifies themselves as Latino or Hispanic. Between 1990 and 2014, the Latino population in New York State has increased 66%, reaching almost 3.7 million (19%) of the population, and most of them live in New York City Metropolitan area.

The Latino Contribution to the United States:

The US Census Bureau (2016), reports that in the State of New York, 83% of Latinos do not speak English in their homes. Lack of English proficiency is a major obstacle for their access to medical and mental health services. Most importantly yet, for those who preferred to get mental health services in Spanish they had less probabilities for access to mental health services. Compared with those Latinos with English proficiency, those with limited knowledge of English were 65 years old or older, with higher probabilities of having medical insurance, all the factors contribute to the risk of emotional stress.

Of the 50 million of Latinos who make the most contribution to the demographic development in the United States continues to be in vast majority, Mexicans, Puerto Ricans and Cubans, but the face of the majority of this country is changing (US Census Bureau,2016). The numbers of the 2010 US Census demonstrate that Latinos are more than 16% of the population and their number is growing to a 43% in the last decade. Latinos contributed between 2000 and 2010 to the 56% of the increased of the total population of this country. The financial recession hit the hardest specially to Latinos with the construction crisis, an important sector of employment for this minority group and only in 2009, 1,4 million Latinos were added to this group of poor people that in the United States is determined by annual salary well below $22,000.

According to the US Census Bureau (2016), the poverty rate among Latinos was 23.4% compared to White people or 12.4%, Afro-Americans 26.2%, Native Americans 27.6%, meanwhile Asians were 12.3%. The level of education of Latinos is notably inferior to the general population, 23.5% of Latinos has completed less of nine years of high school compared to 6.3% of the general population, 3% of White and 5.4% of African Americans. The other extreme of academic education, only 12% of Latinos have graduated from a university, compared to the general population, 31.1% of Whites and 17.7% of African Americans. Although the rhythm of growing of the Latino population has decreased in recent years, the Office of Census calculates that for the year 2050 there will be about 100 million Latinos, this is almost 25% of the general population.

The Case of Peruvians in the United States:

In 2017, 679,340 residents of the United States identified themselves as Peruvians. The Peruvian Americans arrived in the United States in four small waves, that took place first, in San Francisco, California during the search for gold along with Chilean miners, at the beginning of 1848 and in the metropolitan area of Detroit in 1950. The other wave of immigration took place again during the first part of the XX century, due to the expansion of the textile industry in New York and New Jersey. Later, at the beginning of 1970, another wave of Peruvian citizens arrived in the United States, in most part escaping from the military government. The years 1980-1990, were witness to the most important flow of Peruvians in the United States, this time in response to the unstable political government and to a destroyed economy, as well as running away from terrorism. (Office of the US Census Bureau, 2017).

Typically, Peruvians immigrated to the United States for economic reasons, escaping from poverty and in search of a better quality of life. Many Peruvians are from urban zones of Perú, especially from the Capital, Lima. Many of them have settled down in the Metropolitan area of New York City in Queens County. The States with the largest Peruvian population in the United States are Florida, California, New Jersey, and New York. Texas, and Virginia are also home to a significant people of Peruvian descendants.

While this author was attending the Pontific Catholic University in Lima Perú, a national strike of teachers stopped his professional studies. In 1975, he immigrated to the United States and entered Southwestern College in Winfield, Kansas. It was a school of about 800 students, some from different countries, in a town of about ten thousand people. Along with his brother Jorge, they were the only students from Latin America (Perú). While in this college, he lived with an American family who welcomed him into their home. They did not speak Spanish, and his understanding of English was limited. He went through an adjustment process that lasted for a long time. Everything was completely new and different to him, from the food, clothing, and the way of life. He missed his parents, siblings, family, friends, the neighborhood (el barrio), and his favorite foods. Everything had changed and a new life had to begin. The author can understand how other immigrants feel when coming to this country and leaving everything behind to start a new beginning in a different language and a new way of life. Therefore, he can understand and relate to how the Latino and other immigrants feel in this new environment.

Economic Conditions of Peruvians in the United States:

Even though it is a recent ethnic group, the average annual salary of Peruvians meet the average salary of American homes, and 30% of Peruvians older than 25 has a college degree, exceeding the national average of 24% (US Census Bureau (2017).

Ten States of the United States that Have the Highest Percentage of Peruvians:

1. Florida-100,965, or 0.5% of the State's population
2. California-91,511, or 0.2% of the State's population
3. New Jersey-75,869, or 0.9% of the State's population
4. New York-66,318, or 0.3% of the State's population
5. Virginia-29,096, or 0.3% of the State's population
6. Texas-22,605, or 0.1% of the State's population
7. Maryland-18,229, or 0.3% of the State's population

What is Considered Good Health for Latinos?

According to a survey conducted with doctors and Latino patients in New York City, there is a vast disparity among Latino patients and their doctors regarding what they think about having good health. While many Latinos think that their health is good, their doctors disagreed in large numbers (Tallaj, R., M., 2018). And only one third of Latinos think that they do not get the medical attention they need, while two thirds of the doctors think that Latinos have persistent barriers to have access to medical and mental health services. Most medical and mental health problems are left unattended within the Latino community. Smoking, asthma, obesity, diabetes and arterial hypertension, anxiety, and depression, are some of the main health problems, but education in this area is comparable with the seriousness of this issue, and reports about health education are not available in Spanish. Mental health, drug abuse and alcoholism are still being stigmatized. A taboo, for what tends to be treated deficiently, or not treated (Tallaj, R., 2018).

Education:

The level of education of Latinos is much inferior to that of the general population. Among the adult Latinos in New York City, between the ages of 25 and more, 35% did not graduated from high school, compared to the 14% non-adult Latinos. A lower percentage of Latinos compared with non-Latinos have completed college, 16% vs. 42% (US Bureau of Census, 2018). Although the growth rhythm of the Latino population has recently decreased, the US Bureau of Census (2018), estimates that for next 2030 there will be 74.81 million of Latinos in the United States.

The US Bureau of Census (2018) expects the adult Latino population to grow about 55% in the next three decades, compared with the rest of the White population. The adult Latino population has more probabilities of being poor. 24% of adult Latinos (compared with 12% of Whites). Poor health condition appears to attribute to the low financial level and the time exposed to occupations that affect their health (construction, landscaping, carpentry, agriculture, etc.). Putting them together, the access to healthcare services for this population is extremely limited (NKI Center for Excellence in Culturally Competent Mental Health, 2011).

Every year, millions of Americans are affected by emotional problems and Latinos are not an exception. The immigrant Latino population and their children find an alarming number of risks factors and emotional problems. Also, their limited minority condition and citizenship could limit their access to services that they need. According to a report from Zarate, M., (2013), while the emotional problems are the result of a combination of genes and environmental factors, psychosocial circumstances also play an important role.

Children of immigrants could have difficulty living with expectations and demands of a culture in their home and another culture in school. The children may not go to their parents whenever they have problems or worries, thinking that their parents do not understand enough the American culture to be able to help them or may be too stressed due to their settlement. While the second and third generation of immigrants faces higher risks of emotional problems, many Latino immigrants only seek mental health treatment when their condition is worsened. The Latino immigrants are underrepresented in the health and mental health system and in treatment of problems that do not require hospitalization (NKI Center for Excellence in Culturally Competent Mental Health, 2011). This means that frequent doctor's office's do not take care of persons with emotional problems or could have the risk of hurting themselves or others. It Is not helpful that when a person enters a doctor's office suffering from an emotional problem (anxiety/depression), and the first question is; *"do you have medical insurance"? "did you bring your insurance card"?*

Latinos have the highest rate of not having medical insurance among any other group in the United States. Lack of medical insurance prevents the access to medical and mental health services. In 2007, 32% of the Latino population did not have medical insurance compared to the White non-Latino population, 10.4% (Pew Research Center, 2009). The index is higher for older Mexican Americans,37.6% than Puerto Ricans, 20.4%, and Cubans. 22% of younger than 65 do not have medical insurance. Children make 29% of younger than 19 and 8 years old who do not have medical insurance, compared with 11% of Whites of the same age (NKI Center of Excellence in Culturally Competent Mental Health, 2011). The reason for the lack of medical insurance, according to the US Bureau of Census (2018), is because the employers do not offer medical insurance and only 44% of Latinos that have medical insurance is due to citizenship, level of education and characteristics of place of employment.

The level of acculturation among Latinos in the United States could be a factor to predict emotional problems and the evidence of the role of acculturation has been consistent. Ortega, A. N., 2000), reported the possibility of increased of emotional problems and alcohol abuse and substance abuse among Latinos accultured than non-accultured to the United States. The way of living in the United States imposes cultural changes and stress in the way of living of Latinos. Adapting to the American culture could weakness the Latino family structure (familism), because there is not a solid family system and the mental health of parents and their children could worsen (Diaz, C. J., Niño, M., 2019). According to these authors, Latino immigrants have better health and mental health than Latinos who were born in the United States. The strong family orientation, also known as familism, could contribute to their immigrant advantage. Because of the increasing monolingual and bilinguals among the Latino population in the United States, it is important for clinical/psychiatric social workers to be culturally competent and sensitives to be able to obtain positive results. It is this author's opinion that when services are offered in the language of the client/patient without need of a translator, Latinos continue the treatment longer than when the services are not provided in their own language.

Family, Its Importance, and Its Main Socioeconomic Transformations:

Until recently, many Americans agreed that family life was composed of a group of beliefs so scattered that these were accepted as real facts. In the United States, immigrant families must avoid many challenges related to economic sustention, housing, and education for their children. Some obstacles are lack of education, not being able to read or speak English, lack of familiarity with the American way of life, difficulty to find stable employment, or one that pays enough to be able to support the family and the difficulty of having access to public assistance, health and mental health services among others.

In the Latino family, the father is the head of the household, the role model. He transmits strengths, values, and sets example for his children, and when he is gone from home in search of better opportunities, he leaves everything behind. Simply, he is not there at home, with his family. There are many reasons for families to break up or separate, and even though they have links that unite them, there is migration, which is the movement of people from one place to another. It can be temporary or permanent. Migration impacts both the place left behind and, the place where migrants settle. These impacts can be both positive and negative. Some people decide to migrate for different reasons, be these political, financial, educational, or work related. Such is the case of this author who came to the United States to improve his career opportunities. Many times we only talk about the immigrant suffering the separation from his/her family, but what about the suffering of his/her parents, his wife/husband, his/her children, the girlfriend/ boyfriend, the fiancée, his/her friends, his/her siblings, spaces, costumes, the neighborhood, a life, the counterpart, the suffering of the family when they see their son/daughter, friend go away? Because of different reasons, aimlessly, with only a goal or a dream which is what keeps him/her steady in his/her decision to leave, with the disappointment of his/ her country or his/her city, with many injustices, with his/ her family in his/her heart and mind, there is no fear, at least it should not to be mentioned because it weakens.

II.

Needed Mental Health Services

According to a report from the World Health Organization (WHO, 2013), mental health is defined as a state of wellbeing in which the individual is aware of his/hers own capabilities, is capable to face life's stressors, can work productively and capable to contribute to the community. The positive dimension of mental health stands out in the definition of health listed in the Constitution of the World Health Organization (WHO, 2013). Health is a state of complete physical, mental, and social wellbeing, and not the absence of affections or illness. Mental health includes our emotional, psychological, and social wellbeing. It affects the way we think, feel, and behave when facing challenging problems. It also helps to determine how we manage us emotional stress, how we relate with other people and how we make decisions. Mental health is important in all phases of our life from birth to the end of life.

The increase of mental health problems in the Latino community in New York is alarming. It has been exacerbated by current health care problems like Covid-19 (coronavirus).

It is also alarming for Latin America, where the resources are scarce. For this reason, this author suggests that clinical social work in mental health should be expanded, with emphasis in education, promotion, and prevention of mental health problems. Clinical social workers provide mental health services to individuals, groups and families who have emotional problems, through diagnosis and psychotherapy. It is important to note that the actual family context is more complex, due to the way that marital relationships are formalized and ruptured.

The stress of acculturation is particularly difficult for Latino families with parents who are monolingual and with their children who are bilingual and have problems adapting to the American culture. According to a report from the American Psychological Association (2013), titled, "The Psychology of Immigration in the New Century," parents of immigrant Latinos and their children live in different worlds and frequently parents do not know much of what their children do when they are out of their home. This situation puts pressure on their children to look for an exit to their problems and what advice their parents can give to them. Even though there is an increase of need for professional servicers among Latino families and access to professional mental health services, many families do not seek these services due to the stigma they have about mental health problems. The American Psychological Association (2013), recommends that mental health services should be developed in three phases:

1. Cultural knowledge of the psychotherapist.
2. Attitudes and beliefs of the psychotherapist towards the different attitudes of clients/patients.
3. Beliefs of clients/patients and personal understanding, skills of the psychotherapist and adequate therapeutic interventions available. This includes offering to clients/patients, easy access to resources such as, translators and legal aide, as well as facilitating access to different community programs available in the community.

It is also necessary for the interdisciplinary intervention among agencies of the health care system. It is this author's opinion that there should be a transition of collaboration of services without interruption among hospitals, schools, and community mental health centers. By doing so, patients will continue receiving mental health services without delays. The mental health system can also help to improve the mental health of the Latino communities by locating them where they are. There should be information campaigns along with media networks in different languages, in places where the Latino immigrant gather such as, churches, social clubs (American Psychological Association, 2013.

Social work practice with Latinos demands a careful examination of the self and an understanding of how clinical social workers' own worldviews and status vis-a-vis the domain society affect our practice with Latinos. As clinicians therefore we need to be aware of our own conceptualization of a client/patient. For example, if the clinical social worker holds a worldview that values individualism, she/he should critically assess how to approach a client/patient with collectivist worldview. The clinical social worker's self-awareness is critical and involves the development of knowledge regarding cultural heritage and the potential effects of racial and cultural background and history on work with clients/patients (Sue, D. W., et al., 1990).

Interdisciplinary Clinical Social Work:

According to Abramson. J. S., & Mizrahi, T. (1996), Garcés, C. (2018-2019), the reasoning for participation and collaboration among health care professionals is based on the recognition of the complexity of human problems, and the level of knowledge and intervention skills that are needed to obtain positive results. The clinical social worker intensifies the effectiveness of his/her intervention that are necessary to get positive results. The clinical social worker intensifies the effectiveness of his/her intervention by having knowledge of the culture and history of a client/patient. Culture and traditions are important components. It is also important for the client/patient and his/her family to be able to share his/her traditions with the clinical social worker during the initial interview. A good personal question could be: what is important in your culture that would help me to be able to offer my services? The answer to this question could help to prevent misunderstandings between the clinical social worker and the client/patient and family members (Garcés, C., 2018-2919).

Common Mental Health Problems Among the Latino Community in the United States:

Latinos have the same incidence of mental health problems when compared to the rest of the American population. However, certain concerns, experiences, ways of understanding and how to handle them could be different. Without mental health we cannot be healthy. Any part of the human body, including the brain, could get sick. We all go through different events or situations that occasionally can cause emotional ups and downs. Mental health problems go beyond our emotional reactions that we go through during different situations. It has to do with some situations or conditions that could change our routine because these can get complicated and could also create relationship problems with other people, as well as in the work setting and lose employment. Without adequate treatment, mental health problems could get worse and make it difficult the daily life of a person (National Alliance on Mental Illness, 2019).

Symptoms of Emotional Problems:

1. Personality changes.
2. Agitated, aggressive.
3. Withdrawn, low self-esteem, helpless.
4. Racing thoughts, moody, confusion, forgetful, poor concentration, grandiosity, hallucinations, delusions, suicidal.

The Most Common Mental Health Problems in the Latino Community:

1. Schizophrenia.
2. General anxiety disorder.
3. Major depression.
4. Stress disorder.
5. Bipolar disorder.
6. Panic attacks.

Other Problems Associated with Mental Health in the Latino Community:

1. Suicidal attempts.
2. Excessive use of illicit drugs and alcohol.
3. Domestic violence.
4. Child abuse.

Nonetheless, the Latino communities in the United States show a similar predisposition to the mental health problems, when compared to the rest of the population. Sadly, there are many inequalities to mental health and quality of treatment. This inequality exposes a high risk for Latinos of having a mental health breakdown or crisis situations and being able to be treated adequately. Generally, Latinos do not seek mental health treatment. According to the Administration of Substance and Mental Health, in 2012, only 27% of Latinos with mental health related problems sought professional help. Generally, the people in the Latino communities do not talk about their mental health problems. There is not enough information on this issue, and we cannot know what have not been taught. Many Latinos do not seek mental health treatments because they do not recognize the symptoms or because they do not know where to get help. This lack of information exacerbates the stigma already associated with mental health problems. Many Latinos do not seek mental health treatment out fear of being labeled as "crazy," since this could cause them shame.

The stress of acculturation according to Dillon, F., & et.al, (2013), has to do with the psychological stress that is experienced by immigrants when responding to the challenges that they encounter while adjusting to a different culture. Decades of research studies has sparked interest about the impact of mental health problems among Latinos in the United States, making this a frequent determinant of inequalities in mental health services for Latinos. Acculturative stress is linked to multiple psychosocial and mental health problems, including, anxiety, depression, suicide, alcohol, and illegal drug abuse. Despite this, there is not enough understanding about the experiences that are related to acculturative stress during the first years of immigrating to the United States. Acculturative stress can have a negative impact on children's psychological heath (Rogers L-Sirin et al., 2014).

Latinos in the United States face many factors that can increase their risk of mental health problems. Stress could manifest itself through depression and anxiety, which could lead to the use and abuse of illegal drugs and alcohol, and in many instances, in suicide. Stress is also manifested through immigration, which is the cause of emotional distress, and to many immigrants the transition of relocation is problematic. According to Insel, T. R. (2005), the systemic investigation within the moratorium trajectory and the subsequent follow up of the cultural, vocational, social indicators of the family functioning could help clinical social workers to recognize problems, adjustments and to engage in the promotion of mental health, prevention, and treatment interventions in each time. Due to the limited evidence of studies, more research, would help to evaluate intervention strategies for the promotion of mental health in the Latino communities for the prevention of mental health problems that respond to problems of acculturation.

Cultural differences could be the cause for clinical social workers to incorrectly diagnose their clients/patients. For example: Latinos usually describe their symptoms that are related to depression with "nervousness, fatigue, or physically ill." These symptoms are related to depression. However, when the clinical social worker does not understand the client's/patient's culture, this too could influence the treatment negatively, and not be able to recognize the symptoms of depression. Even though Latinos prefer to be treated by Latino mental health professionals, unfortunately this is not always possible due to the small percentage of Latino clinical social workers or bilingual clinical social workers who are culturally competent. To understand the reasons for cultural disparities, it will help us to build a mental health system that can be able to combine the superior quality of effective mental health services. Latinos conform one third of the eight million habitants of New York City. But even when representing a substantial part of the State of New York, and no sooner we are an increasing population, they keep themselves invisible. Latinos are invisible because they are different, and with these factors together, the attention of health and mental health services are in crisis. Compared with New York residents. Latino immigrants lack health care benefits and lack medical care. Latino immigrants face obstacles that make them more at risk of getting sick (Tallaj, R.M., 2018).

Both, the presentation of emotional problems and the way they are explained by Latinos in the United States are different. According to Lewis-Fernandez, E, et al. (2005), Latinos with depression problems have more probabilities of presenting themselves with psychosomatic complaints when compared with White Americans. This could be the reason that Latinos have more probabilities to seek medical treatment for these problems, instead of seeking mental health treatment. It is important that the somatic presentation of depression among Latinos could make doctors to make mistakes, ending up with a wrong diagnosis, unnecessary medical exams, and inadequate treatment (Lewis-Fernandez, et al., 2005).

Based on the author's professional experiences in the hospital and community mental health settings since 1985 to this date, Latinos have different ways of believing about their emotional problems. Many Latinos believe in spirits or sins for the cause of their illness; an interpretation that to this date may not be understood by mental health care professionals. They may use different language that prevents recognition and understanding of their problems. Lack of success to adequately distinguish common emotional cultural problems could contribute to the delay in seeking help for their problems, inadequate treatment, and negative results.

A known cultural disorder among Latinos is "nervous attack" which is a language of desperation that is particularly common among Latinos from the Caribbean and is well recognized by many Latinos. This is described in the Diagnostic Criteria of The DSM-5 (2013) of cultural disorders and the symptoms include: Uncontrolled chills, crying attacks, body shakes, heat in the chest area to the head, turning verbally or physically aggressive. Typically, nervous attack occurs because of a stress event, especially related to family problems. Frequently, the nervous attack is common for the person to suffer amnesia of what took place, but soon after returns to his/her normal functioning. The nervous attack is often compared with an episode of panic attack due to the similarity of the symptoms. Both panic attacks and nervous attacks have a close association with the absence of symptoms of fear and panic (Guarmaccia, P.J., 2008). Because nervous attack is described as a temporary emotional reaction to circumstances of daily life, the person could not recognize the debilitating emotional problem or the need to seek professional mental health services (NKI Center for Excellence in Culturally Competent Mental Health, 2009).

While the fear symptoms are like the ones in the DSM-5 Diagnostic and Statistical Criteria Manual of Mental Disorders (2013), the complications for its treatment are different. Traditionally, the treatment for fear consists of a practice of cultural rituals, with the purpose of calling the soul to come back to the body to "clean" the affected person and return the total balance to his/her body. Such rituals are known by the traditional Latin medicine man. While those clients/patients who suffer from fear can experience some improvement in the conventional treatment for symptoms of major depression, lack of consideration of the cultural beliefs of clients/patients could limit the efficiency of the therapeutic intervention, affect the adherence and modify the trust (or lack of trust) in the sector of formal mental health. The event that precipitates fear could be correlative with the western differential diagnosis. For example, fear because of a conflict of a major correlation with the western differential diagnosis of major depression disorder (Guarmaccia, P. J., 2008).

The challenges are even greater for people who do not speak English when having to go to an interview with the clinical social worker about their feelings in their own language with the assistance of a translator. The translation can be helpful, but the clinical social worker should have good understanding of the cultural context to be able to help the client/patient. Different dialects could also complicate the translation. Many Latino immigrants rather not seek professional mental health help or trust non-Spanish speaking clinical social workers due to the lack of cultural understanding and the professional competency to understand their problems. According to The National Alliance on Mental Health (2017), one of five Latinos suffer from a mental health problem. Latinos have a collective orientation, being family orientated (familism), of mutual help and united, this are family ties of the Latino culture (National Alliance on Mental Health, 2011). Familism is a unique word in the Spanish language that emphasizes a strong family relationship, which could help as a protective factor that promotes social support which protects people against symptoms of depression, including high risk environmental situations (National Alliance on Mental Health, 2011).

Depression in the Latino Woman:

Even though major depression in the Latin woman is being recognized, the risk and the mechanisms of protection that are associated with the effects in children when the mother suffers from depression, is well understood by Latino families.

During the 2000 census, Latin women were 51% of the Latino population in the United States (Bureau of Census, 2000). Most Latino women are concentrated in occupations of low salaries, they work in factories, restaurants, house cleaning, hair salons, as receptionists, laundry shops, flower shops, farms. The Latino women have double unemployment when compared with Caucasian American women, and suffer multiple social and economic disadvantages such as, low level of education, unemployment, low income. They may be single mothers, have high levels of poverty and may be victims of domestic violence. These factors affect their mental health and limit their access to health and mental health care services. Latino women who are born in the United States have a higher risk level of major depression and suicide attempts than the non-Latino women (Gia Chello, A., 2001). The prevalence of depression in Latino women is higher (46%) than in Latino men (19%). The National Alliance on Mental illness (2016).

A study by Lewis. M. J. et al. (2005) found significant levels of stigma associated to symptoms of depression and antidepressant medication. Latinos who participated in the study and received treatment for depression said that an experience with depressive symptoms is described negatively, seen as a characteristic within the social context. When the same people were interview about the complications adhering to antidepressant medication therapy, 73% of participants made comments with reference to stigma, antidepressant medication, followed by 87% of side effects from the medication. Having to take antidepressant medication appears to be disapproved by families of the participants and of their social system support. It is seen as they see it as a sign of weakness.

Mental Health Services vs. Home Remedy (Botanicals)

The low index of utilizing mental health services among the Latino population is attributed to the social consequences of seeking these services. The study suggests that Latinos do not seek help due to fear of deportation, mistrust of providers and fear of authorities (Lewis, M.J., et al., 2005). Other studies suggest that people are afraid to bring shame to the family when seeking mental health services. According to the same study Latinos see emotional problems as something very private and it should not be shared with others outside the family. Latinos can be less ready and fit than White Americans in seeking mental health services because their mental health is supported by the family. Social resources include family, friends, godparents, religious affiliations, spiritual and other people who practice healings and groups of personal help. These resources are frequently used instead of professional mental health services; however, literature suggests that these resources do not effectively replace professional services.

Botanical stores (ethnical stores of home remedies) are particularly located in New York City. These types of stores offer religious home remedies, spiritual products, and services to a diverse clientele who are mostly from Latin America and the Caribbean countries. The presence of botanicals in New York City is related to the presence of dispensaries (drugstores that appeared in 1900). They are in areas were Latinos are the majority. Also, the Botanical offers counseling services to people who seek spiritual and emotional guidance in a variety of situations, from financial to emotional problems (counseling). The perception of the effectiveness of home practice, combined with medicinal herbs that are offered in the botanic are cheap (low cost), and of easy access, bring Latinos who seek informal mental health services (Gómez, A., Beloz, J., et al (2011).

In a recent study by Perez Porto, M (2017-2019), medicine men are said to be able to cure a wide variety of physiological, spiritual, and emotional sufferings. They also said to have a unique way to diagnose and to cure, compared to the model of the United States: Psychosomatic causes which are the result of social demand. Latinos with physical and emotional problems have the tendency to make less use of mental health services than White Americans. In 2007, only 26.6% of Latinos with serios mental health problems received services, compared with 50% of White Latinos.

Required Credentials to Practice Clinical Social Work in the United States:

1. Licensed Clinical Social Worker (LCVSW)
2. Licensed Master Social Worker (LMSW)
3. Licensed Marital Family Therapist) LFT)
4. Licensed Counselor in Mental Health (LMHC)
5. Licensed in Professional Counseling (LPC)
6. PhD in Social Work

New Emergency Services Station.

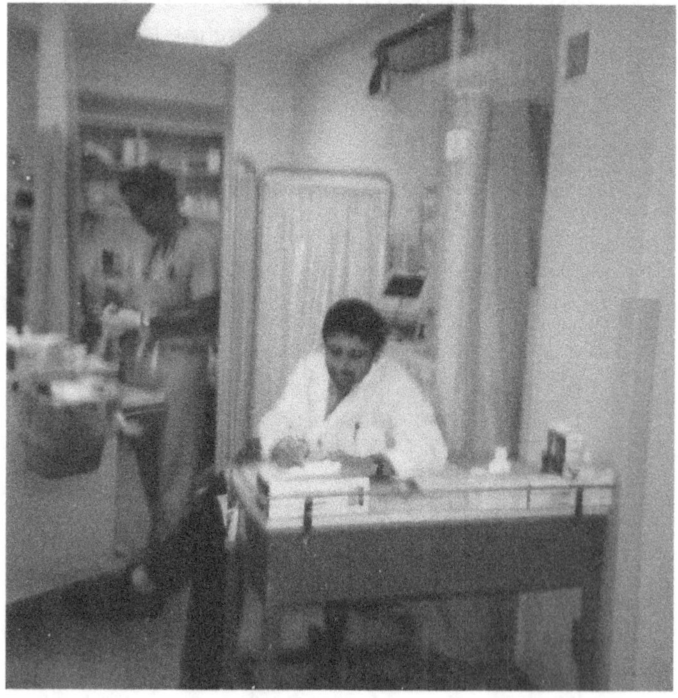

III.

Social Work in Mental Health

Because of the expansion of social work practice in hospitals, social workers had to find new roles for themselves, many decided to enter areas of mental health and make themselves useful in this regard. This promotion in mental health has a history (National Institute of Mental Health, 1991). From psychiatry hospitals to the development of community mental health centers, social workers have found themselves providing psychotherapy to individuals, groups, and families. Also, social workers have been active in the actual prevention of mental illness caused by current world events like Covid-19. They have made efforts to develop public programs and allocate funds, to make sure that mental illness is treated with the same degree of gravity as other medical illnesses.

By working with other mental health professionals (psychologists, psychiatrists), social workers began to collaborate in the development of theories of ethology and interventions, which have been now tried through practice and research. However, unbeknown to the unsuspecting investigator, emphasis on mental health instead of the social environment has changed the historical course of the typical social worker. Instead of the individual and his environment, the clinical social worker seeks to justify practice on the same grounds as the medical doctor or nurse, who subscribes to the bio-psychosocial approach to the consumer. This may seem like a small detail in a large panoramic view of the place of the clinical social worker in society, but it is not a small gnat or flies in the ointment. Now clinical social workers work on the psyche of the individual, helping his/her to find happiness, peace inside of him/herself and to better their mental health.

The main objective of clinical social workers in mental health is to be able to help people who suffer from mental illness, so that they can function in the world in which they live. This new adopted role has helped to improve the conditions for the mentally ill, who are no longer locked up in psychiatric institutions. The concept subscribed to now be the clinical social worker helps the consumer "adjust" to the realities of life (National Institute of Mental Health, 1991).

Unlike the psychiatrists, the clinical social workers are trained to have interest in the whole person. Yet, these new adopted roles and environments are challenging, for the medical model is hard to squash. It prevails, and this means that the clinical social worker's training to treat the whole person bumps head-on into psychiatry's focus, which is to cure the illness by prescribing psychotropic medication (National Institute of Mental Health, 1991). What this really means is even the adopted role of the clinical social worker, to be the advocate for the mentally ill has also been challenged as well. The typical clinical social worker in a psychiatric hospital or a community mental health clinic has his/her hands tied to the psychiatrist who may not really believe that psychotherapy conducted by a clinical social worker helps the patient as much as an anti-psychotic medication. If this is true, it might have been wiser for the clinical social worker to remain in the hospital setting,

This author's professional experience in community mental health began after graduating from Fordham University in 1985. It was in the Puerto Rican Family Institute in the South Bronx, New York, where he first worked as a psychiatric social worker. The people in the South Bronx were mainly Puerto Ricans, from the Dominican Republic and from other countries of Latin America. Later, in 1997 he went to work at Flushing Hospital Outpatient Psychiatric Clinic, and at Queens Neuropsychiatric Institute in Jackson Heights Queens, New York where most of the clients/ patients were from Perú, Chile, Argentina, Ecuador, Bolivia, México, Colombia, Uruguay, and Venezuela. Since 2010 he has been working as a psychotherapist at Community Counseling Services on Long island, New York where the clients/patients are mixed; Americans and Latinos mostly from Central America; Honduras, El Salvador, Guatemala, Nicaragua, and México.

According to a report from the World Health Organization (WHO, 2013), mental health is defined as a state of wellbeing in which an individual is aware of his/her own capabilities, is capable to face normal life's stressors, can work productively and capable to contribute to the community. The positive dimension of mental health stands out in the definition of health listed in the Constitution of the World Health Organization (WHO, 2013): Health is a state of complete physical, mental, and social wellbeing. It affects the way we think, feel, and behave when facing challenging problems. It also helps to determine how we manage emotional stress, how we relate with other people and how we make decisions. Mental health is important in all phases of our life from birth to the end of life.

Understanding Clinical Social Work:

Clinical social work is a type of specialty of medical social work, which deals with counseling, psychotherapy, and coordinating services (discharge planning) to individuals with severe emotional problems, and in some situation needed psychiatric hospitalization or other psychiatric treatment. Clinical social workers have a variety of tasks when treating clients/patients, including but not limited to psychosocial evaluations, individual, family and group psychotherapy, crisis intervention, emotional support, and coordinating medical attention and discharge planning. Clinical social workers are employed in a variety of settings: Hospitals, court system, schools, drug and rehabilitation centers, nursing and rehabilitation centers, community mental health centers (NASW, 2016).

Clinical Social Workers Can Work As:

1. Administrators of mental health clinics
2. Researchers

3. Psychiatric and medical hospitals
4. Case managers (child abuse and neglect, domestic violence, elderly abuse).
5. Psychotherapist

Clinical Social Work is a Specialty that Meets the Following Requirements (NASW, 2016):

1. Has a systemic body of theories that supports what it does
2. Has professional authority emanating from the domain of theory
3. Has community knowledge that the profession is valid
4. Has a code of ethics that governs the conduct of its members, has a professional culture within a vocabulary, and professional methodology

Clinical social work bases its methodology in the systemic field of evidence based in knowledge derived from research and practical evaluation, including its own knowledge and a specific content. It also acknowledges the complex interactions among people and their environment, and the capacity of individuals to react when they are affected by multiple influences or circumstances upon themselves, including psychosocial, health and environmental factors such as the Cvid-19. The social work profession extracts from theories of human development, social theory, and social systems theory to analyze complex situations, and familiarize individual changes of cultural and social organizations (NASW Definition of Social Work, 2000).

Clinical social workers provide mental health services (psychotherapy) to individuals, families, and groups of individuals who have emotional problems. Clinical social workers provide psychotherapy and diagnose emotional problems by using the DSM-5 Diagnostic and Statistical Manual of Mental Disorders (2013).

The role of the social worker varies according of the setting of practice. In the hospital setting is mostly discharge planning. This starts as soon as the patient is admitted to the hospital and takes place upon the patient's discharge from the hospital. Sometimes patients need special services such as, referrals to nursing and rehabilitation nursing homes, orthopedic rehabilitation, drug, and alcohol rehabilitation (Garcés, C., 2018-2019). During the discharge planning, the clinical social worker must make sure that the patient has all the necessary resources before going back home and to be able to function in the community. Presently, hospital stay is shorter than a few years ago (Garcés, C., 2018-2019., NASW, 2016).

Psychiatric Social Work:

Psychiatric social work started in 1907, almost simultaneously with hospital social work in John Hopkins Hospital in Boston. Garnet I. Pelton was the first social worker in 1907 and was assigned to the hospital's dispensary, known as Community Mental Health Center. Two years later, Margaret Brogen, a nurse assumed the position and worked alone for several years. After all it became obvious to the hospital's administrators that her services were priceless, and the hospital would benefit by having more social workers to take care of patients. The department of social work in the hospital became a formal part of the hospital in 1912, after the hospital started to hire more social workers. At that time, social work education was in its early stages and most of the social workers were trained by nurses (NASW, 2007).

Psychiatric social work is a specialty of social work and follows the rehabilitation and restructuration of a patient's personality (takes place in psychiatric hospitals, community mental health centers, etc.), and psychosocial prophylaxis which deals with human mismatches. Psychiatric social work is the work of research about mental health problems, undertaking direct and responsible intervention along with psychiatry, with the objective to help patients who suffer from emotional problems. The psychiatric social worker is a professional who contributes to the prevention, treatment, and rehabilitation of emotional problems working for it with the client/patient, his/her family with the objective to achieve social restoration.

The first psychiatric social workers had the support of Dr. Meyer from the Massachusetts General Hospital, who as well as Dr. Richard Cabot in 1905, understood that psychosocial factors had much to do with the genetics of emotional problems, and the social force could be introduced to improve their mental health. Dr. Meyer's wife, Mary Brooks Meyer, worked as a psychiatric social worker before she arrived at Baltimore. In her first position at the Pathologic Institute at New York Hospital in New

York City, Ms. Meyer Brooks had already visited the homes of her patients and reported their conditions of their homes to her husband. (NASW, 2007).

Psychiatric social workers work in psychiatric hospitals and community mental health clinics. Among other missions of psychiatric social work in the field of psychiatry there is:

1. The prevention of emotional problems through anticipated detection of susceptible cases.
2. The explanation to users of mental health services.
3. Implementation of measurements to improve follow up treatment such as, organizing family groups, self-help, collaboration in mental health awareness campaigns.

The Psychiatric Social Worker:

Is a trained professional who evaluates and generates changes in the person who goes to his/her office for consultation and psychotherapy, which is given with the purpose to improve the quality of life through changes in the behavior and attitudes. The psychiatric social worker makes use of the DSM-5 Diagnostic and Statistical Manual of Mental Health (2013), for the evaluation of emotional problems. The psychiatric social worker is a licensed clinical social worker, who helps people to improve their lives, develop better cognitive and emotional skills, reduce symptoms of emotional distress to be able to face adversities. This professional is a person who help people to remember that they are valued and appreciated by others too.

The Psychiatric Social Worker as a Family Psychotherapist:

1. Educates family members about the role of the family as a group, particularly, how they function among themselves.
2. Helps the family to focus less on the member who was identified as "problematic," and to focused more on the family as a unit.
3. Helps to identify conflicts and anxieties as well as to work together to develop strategies to solve them.
4. Strengthens all family members to be able to work together to solve problems.
5. Teaches ways to solve problems and changes within the family. Sometimes, the way that family members solve their problems makes them to have more probabilities to develop depressive symptoms.

Practice Models of Clinical/Psychiatric Social Work (NASW, 2014):

1. **Resolution of problems.** The focus of this model is the understanding of the problem, searching for different ideas to solve the problem, allowing the client/patient to find a solution, to try the solution, and later, evaluate the outcome of the solution.
2. **Focus on homework.** The focus of this model is to separate the problem in small areas that the client/ patient can achieve. The clinical social worker can use this as a practice, date limit and contract, to

help the client/patient to be able to feel successful and motivated to solve the problem.

3. **Focus on the solution.** The focus of this model is to start with the solution, later to help the client/patient to stablish steps to arrive to the solution of the problem.

4. **Narrative.** The focus of this model is in using words and other models to help the client/patient to empower his/her life.

5. **Cognitive psychotherapy (CPT).** This model combines cognitive psychotherapy with behavioral psychotherapy, identifying inadequate patterns of the thinking process, and emotional answers, or behavior, substituting them with desirable patterns of thinking, emotional answers, or behavior. How to control anxiety and stress? Learning techniques of relaxation such as, deep breathing, talking out loud and saying: "I did this before," and distractions, identifying situations that are frequently avoided, and gradually getting closer to fearful situations.

Clinical social work is important because of the skills of its practitioners to be able to adapt to different settings and functions, including head of team members in multidisciplinary centers and in community mental health centers. Clients/patients, individuals, couples, families, children and groups, benefit from a wide variety of direct services including but not limited to psychosocial evaluations, treatment plans, crisis intervention, and case management.

The skillful and flexible application of knowledge, theories, and methods of intervention with the psychosocial focus, is a seal of quality of clinical social work. The direct process of interventions from person/people, are conducted with people of all ages and of natural differences, from prevention services, crisis interventions, psychoeducational, up to the defense of the rights of clients/patients, as well as the extensive process of psychotherapy. Most often, clinical social workers supervise and consult with other colleagues and can also participate in direct and indirect practice (administration, research, writing). It is a practice standard for clinical social workers to continue clinical education and adhere to the professional code of ethics (Center for Clinical Social Work Research, 2007.

Social Work in the Hospital Center:

Social work was introduced to the hospitals in the United States by Dr. Richard Cabot in 1905. Dr. Cabot created the first position of social work in the world, given it first to Garmet Pelton, and later was followed by Ida Cannon (Davidson, K., 1998). In 1918, The National Association of Social Workers (NASW), was established with the purpose to improve the relation between formal education and practice in hospitals. The role of the social workers was to provide social services to those people in need, however the administrators only wanted for the social workers to evaluate the social needs of patients to give relieve to the doctors, and to avoid the abuse of the hospital by the patients (Davidson, K., 1990).

The Social Worker in the Hospital Setting:

1. **Communicates,** emphasizes communication between the medical personnel, patients, and their families, and makes sure that that their medical needs are met.
2. **Offers emotional support,** focusing on psychosocial issues and the emotional needs of patients and their families.
3. **Advocates,** for the patient's rights making sure that the hospital provides quality medical services.
4. **Links,** making sure that the available resources for the patients are adequate.
5. **Advices,** personalizing interactions and understands feelings attitudes and behaviors of patients and their families.
6. **Intervenes,** between patients, families, and medical personnel.
7. Coordinates: organizing services for patients upon their discharge from the hospital.
8. **Educates,** transmitting knowledge, and teaching about the patients' rights including medical decisions, and end of life issues

Based on the author's 24 years of professional experience in the hospital setting (1989-2013), and community mental health settings (1985-present), social workers do little or nothing to promote themselves and their clinical services. The skills, abilities and contributions are not evident to clinical social workers themselves. For instance, the clinical social worker may not know that it takes skills to be in a room with a suffering patient even though the clinical social worker has received years of training. All the years of education training, however, go to the wayside when the clinical social worker is questioned out his/her unique skill set in this example of the suffering patient. This is odd; for doctors and nurses know what their skill set is in this instance. As pointed out by Davidson (1990), and Cowless, L. A. (2000), hospital social work has developed a font of knowledge and has influenced patient care by promoting recognition of the psychosocial component of health care. Social workers in health care settings bring a person and family-centered model of care to assessment and treatment, which differs from the patient-focused medical model (Garcés, C., 2019).

The author's professional experience as a social worker in the hospital setting began in 1989 at Bronx Lebanon Hospital Center in the South Bronx, New York, which is one of the poorest neighborhoods in the United States and is composed of people from almost all over the world. Also, the people of the South Bronx suffer from multiple medical problems, namely asthma, diabetes, Aids, cholesterol, hypertension, and obesity. There are also psychosocial and mental health problems such as, delinquency, drug and alcohol abuse, prostitution, homelessness, child and elderly abuse, domestic violence (Office of Census of the United State, 2006).

Clinical social workers work in hospitals, educating the medical staff about discharge planning, crisis interventions, hospice and palliative care, uniting patients, and families with available community resources. Clinical social workers collaborate with physicians and nurses and other medical staff (Mizrahi, T., Abramson, J., 1985., Garcés, C., 2002), to identify the social needs of patients, not just the presenting problem. While the time of home visits is part of the past, clinical social workers continue participating in evaluations of family situations, reinforcing social supports that are available for those patients who are discharge from the hospital and are in need of continuing of care Garcés, C., 2002-2019). The clinical social worker contributes to the overall operation of the hospital setting by helping/assisting patients and their families cope with crisis, including death and with the discharge planning process from the hospital.

The Clinical Hospital Social Worker:

1. Assesses the social environmental problems of patients.
2. Helps/assists patients to examine possible solutions to their social-environmental problems.
3. Contact community agencies to request services for their social-environmental problems of patients.
4. Inform patients of how their medical problems may create social-environmental problems for them.
5. Refers patients to appropriate hospital personnel for assistance with their social-environmental problems.

During the pandemic of the Covid-19, clinical social workers were performing their clinical roles with the discharge process outside the hospital, in their homes. Doctors and nurses required continued direct contact with patients. Because of the pandemic, hospitals had to reduce the amount of personnel who were considered "essential," among them were social workers. These regulations were imposed by the federal and local governments. The clinical social workers were not able to directly communicate with patients with Covid-19 and their families because of this mandate. Discharge planning is provided via telehealth session with patients and families.

A clinical social worker is a professional who holds a Master's or Doctor's degree in social work from an accredited school of social work. In addition to at least two years of post-master's supervised experience in a clinical setting. The social worker must be licensed, certified, or registered at the clinical level in the jurisdiction of practice. A clinical social worker provides direct services, including intrapsychic dynamics, and life management issues. Clinical social work services are based on biopsychosocial perspectives. Services consist of diagnosis, treatment (including psychotherapy and counseling), client centered advocacy, consultation, evaluation, and prevention of mental illness, emotional or behavioral disturbances.

Clinical Social Workers Can Work As:

1. Administrators in community mental health clinics
2. Researchers
3. Rehabilitators
4. In medical and psychiatric hospitals
5. Case managers
6. Psychotherapists

Clinical Social Work is a Specialty that Meets the Following Requirements:

1. Has a systematic body of theories that sustains its work.
2. Has professional authority that emanates from the domain of theory.
3. Has community recognition that the profession is valid.
4. Has a code of ethics that governs the behavior of its members.
5. Has a consistent professional culture and professional vocabulary and methodology.

Clinical social work bases its methodology on the knowledge derived from research and practice evaluation, including its own knowledge with a specific content. Also, recognizes the complexity of interactions between people and their environment, and the capacity of people to react to multiple influences or circumstances upon themselves, including psychosocial health or environmental factors such as the Covid-19. Social work extracts from theories of human development, social and systems theories to analyze complex situations to get acquainted with individual changes within social and cultural organizations (NASW-Definition of Social Work, 2000).

The Clinical Social Worker as Family Psychotherapist:

1. Teaches to all family members about how family's function in general, and how they work themselves.
2. Helps the family to focus less on the member that was identified as "problematic" and to focus more on the family.
3. Helps to identified conflicts and anxieties, also helps the family to develop strategies to solve them.
4. Strengthens all members to be able to work together in solving their problems.
5. Teaches ways to solve conflicts and changes within the family. Sometimes, the way members solve their problems makes them to have more probabilities to develop depressive symptoms.

The knowledge base of clinical social work includes the theories of biology, psychological and sociological development, diversity and cultural competency, interpersonal relationships, family and group dynamics, emotional problems, addictions, impact of emotional problems on people, traumas. These knowledges are encouraged in the graduate schools of social work and are integrated in the skills of direct practice which are developed by the students for about two years of experience postgraduate under the supervision of a clinical social worker. This period of training is sufficient to prepare the clinical social worker to be able to practice in an autonomous way with license from the State as a clinical social worker. In the following years after graduation, clinical social workers can obtain a generalized advanced practice or can also decide to specialize in one or more areas.

Clinical social work is important because of the skills of its practitioners to adapt to different roles, including department heads in multidisciplinary centers, in hospitals (medical/psychiatric), and in community mental health centers. Clients/patients, individuals, couples, families, children the elderly, and groups benefit from a wide variety of direct services that are provided by clinical social workers, including psychosocial evaluations, treatment, crisis intervention, and case management. The skillful application of knowledge, theories, and methods of intervention, with the biopsychosocial approach, is a quality seal of clinical social work. The interventions of direct process from person/people, are conducted with people of almost all ages and different by nature, from preventive services, crisis intervention and psychoeducational services to the defense of patients' rights, as well as the short or extensive process of counseling and psychotherapy. Typically, clinical social workers supervise and consult with other colleagues and can also participate in direct and indirect practice (administration, research, writing). This is a practice norm for clinical social workers to participate and to continue a long and extensive career to continue their clinical education and adhere to the professional code of ethics (Center for Clinical Social Work Research, 2014).

Psychotherapy Definition:

Greshton (2016), defines psychotherapy to the use of psychosocial methods within a professional relationship, assisting to a person or persons to reach a better psychosocial adjustment modifying their internal and external conditions that affect individuals, groups, and communities, with regard to behavior, feelings, thinking, and interpersonal and intrapersonal processes. social workers and psychotherapists have almost the same roles.

Social work profession has evolved from philanthropy and the welfare theory to social technology, in recent terms, is considered as a scientific discipline in the development of social sciences, that guides a profession with a define space in the satisfaction of human needs, existentially (material), and appreciatively (affective and political). Clinical social work is reinventing and having meaning with respect to a holistic vision of its reality (NASW, 2014). With the arrival of globalization of financial markets, scientific and technological advance, clinical social workers ought to be thinking from a more comprehensive and interdisciplinary dimension, with new methods of intervention, where we can improve the welfare and wellbeing of people, families, and society.

Nonclinical Social Work:

The non-clinical social worker can incorporate psychotherapy in public or private organizations, and in case management. Many times, non-clinical social workers can work providing counseling and helping clients in finding employment, coordinating rehabilitation programs, prevention of child abuse/elderly abuse and neglect programs. Typically, this practice makes them work with clients based in consultation (NASW, 2014).

A Psychotherapist, Clinical Social Worker Is the Same as a Counselor?

When people talk about psychotherapy, they usually refer this term to psychotherapist, clinical social worker, psychologist, counselor within the context of working with people to improve their mental health problems. These terms have the same meaning and can be exchanged. The use of the term over others is only about preference. Counselor and counseling are more common than psychotherapy and psychotherapist in the United States (NASW, 2014).

A list of different terms that Latinos in New York use as a synonymous of psychotherapy:

1. Counselor.
2. Mental health counselor.
3. Psychologist.

Psychotherapist, the meaning is the same, but people refer it to therapy, this is a short version, and has better use than psychotherapy.

How are Emotional Problems Diagnosed?

According to the Desk Reference to the Diagnostic Criteria (DSM-5 (2013):

1. A medical history of the client/patient is necessary.
2. Physical exam and lab work.

3. Psychiatric, psychological, psychosocial evaluation,
    which has questions about thoughts, feelings, and
    behavior.

Wrong Ideas About What is Meant by Psychotherapist:

To better understand what it means a psychotherapist, first
we must talk about what is not. There are many ideas and
wrong concepts about the meaning of psychotherapist. Here
some of them:

1. **Wrong Ideas: The clinical social worker/
    psychotherapist is like a friend to whom people
    pay to listen:** To think that the clinical social
    worker/psychotherapist is a friend who is hired,
    discounts the amount of education and professional
    training that is required to better the mental health
    of people that we serve. Most clinical social workers/
    psychotherapists have six years of education. Others
    have more than a decade of professional studies.

2. **Wrong Ideas: The clinical social worker/
    psychotherapist tells people what to do:** Most
    clinical social workers/psychotherapists do not tell
    anybody what they must do. They are not like
    parents, teachers, or trainers. They do not dictate or
    yell instructions to follow. Clinical social workers/
    psychotherapists work with people to whom they
    teach skills to be able to live a healthy life and be

able to make good decisions. Clinical social workers/psychotherapists empower people and try not to create dependency.

3. **Wrong Ideas: The clinical social worker/psychotherapist, reads the mind:** The clinical social worker/psychotherapist does not try to guess what the client/patient is thinking or analyzes his/her ideas. The main concern of the clinical social worker/psychotherapist is in what the client/patient is thinking, only because wants to help.

Five Theories that Describe the Clinical Social Work Practice (Engard, B., 2017).

1. **Psychosocial Theory.** Its focus is on the way that people are molded and how they react to their environment.
2. **Psychodynamic Theory.** Tries to understand the behavior of people.
3. **Transpersonal Theory.** Was influenced by Carl Jung, uses positive influences, instead of human illnesses, and defenses for the realization human potential. This theory uses saints, artists, heroes, and other similar figures. People who have a good ego can try to emulate as role models and aspirations.
4. **Learning Cognitive Theory:** Its focus is on the effects of the environment, and reinforces behavior, however, Bandura, A. (1977) added two important dimensions: Mediating forces follow between the

stimulus and the answer, and people can learn
behavior trough observation.

5. **Systems Theory:** Claims that behavior is
influenced by a variety of factors that work together
as a system. Parents, friends, school, social status,
home environment, and other factors influence how
a person thinks and behaves.

Ethical and Professional Value/Professional Relationships:

According to the National Association of Social Workers
(NASW,2016), code of ethics are standards of moral
behavior for a society or group, such as social workers. The
code of ethics for a profession has standards of behavior for a
certain profession. These ethical codes reflect concerns and
define basic principles that helps as a professional guidance.
Its purpose is:

1. Provides a practical position to help professionals in
making decisions towards clients/patients and society.
   a. Guarantees society that the professionals are
   going to demonstrate sensibility with respect to
   social expectations.
   b. Guarantees the professionals respect of their
   integrity and freedom.
   c. Assists in clarifying responsibilities that the
   professionals have towards the clients/patients.

Social Workers need to Evaluate their Ethical Practice in the Following Considerations:

    a. The professional moral judgement (do not make the client/patient uncomfortable).
    b. Legal aspects (laws that govern).
    c. Ethical implications (apply ethical principles that should be respected).

2. **The code of ethics is divided in five sections:**
    a. The main objective is to help people in need and to focus on their problems.
    b. Social justice; challenging social injustice.
    c. Dignity and courage of the person. Respect for the individual.
    d. Importance of human relationships.
    e. Integrity; practice within the area of expertise and commitment to better professional skills.

To Remember and Consider:

1. The needs of clients/patients.
2. Level of professional competency of the clinical social worker.
3. Clinical orientation of the clinical social worker.
4. Cultural competence of the clinical social worker with the client/patient.
5. Clinical social workers should respect the code of professional ethics.

Advantages of Being Bilingual/Multicultural:

This author believes that being bilingual (Spanish/English) and multicultural is an advantage, as it better equips him with not only language skills but also with social skills needed to work with others from varying cultures and ethnic backgrounds. Such skills include the ability to be more perceptive to others, to be more empathetic and to communicate more effectively in their own language.

IV.

Conclusion and Recommendations

For the past 35 years, this author has been doing a sustained work in terms of clinical/psychiatric social work in the field of health and mental health. He has an extensive working experience in the hospital and community mental health settings with people of different multicultural and ethnic backgrounds. As a psychotherapist, he can identify the major emotional problems, including crisis precipitants, encourage and exploration of feelings and emotions, generate and explore alternatives and coping strategies and restore functioning through the implementation of plans.

Social work is a profession that is advancing in a way that governments and employers around the world are acknowledging the tremendous impact that clinical social workers have with people they work in their communities. Less crime, better results in medical and mental health system, more people having access to employment and education are the result of social work, supporting for people to have control of their own future and make reality their aspirations. As a profession based on human rights, social work has an essential role in society advocating for communities to raise their voices and defend their rights along with others. The strength of the profession lies in its capacity to build participatory democracy, uniting communities in sustainable futures and to defend human rights.

As clinical social workers we have an important role thus, raising the voices of people whose worries are not always heard proportioned. People outside the social work profession have the possibility of not being familiarized or informed about the psychotherapeutic services that a clinical social worker provides. Lack of knowledge and understanding of what clinical social workers do in the hospital setting and in community mental health centers do, could create conflicts in the collaboration with other professionals in providing clinical services. The efficient intervention of clinical social workers depends in part, on how other health care professionals and the public perceive the role of the clinical social worker. The modern clinical social work must adapt to the globalized world, were the institutions are impacting the unilateral rules and its practice. The progressive increase of different social cultural consumers, especially in hospitals and community mental health centers, constitute a challenge for clinical social workers.

As social workers, we help people to receive quality care and needed resources to live quality life. Assisting children with special needs in schools, assisting people with terminal illness, with changes in their everyday live, and providing needed psychotherapy services to people with emotional problems. We serve society in many ways. While it is a requirement, the use of techniques to help people with diverse medical, psychological, and psychosocial problems, as clinical social workers we could benefit by making use of the holistic approach.

Anxiety and depression around the world have increased due to the pandemic of Covid-19 (Coronavirus), which has brought in fear and uncertainty among the population. For people with mental health problems, there is a risk of increase of these conditions. Now that some places have been opening to the public (shopping malls, restaurants, stores, etc.), people are returning to their "normal way of life." However, those people with emotional problems could face serious problems adjusting. *How can they go through the challenges of continuing their daily lives? How family and friends could help them? How we as clinical social workers could help them?*

The challenge for clinical social workers is to be able to demonstrate our professional and clinical skills, to be able to better the emotional and social wellbeing of the people we serve. As clinical social workers we should contribute in initiatives of research, not only to be able to demonstrate our efficiency in the psychotherapeutic interventions', but also to promote knowledge and understanding among other colleagues about the importance of identifying and communicating the psychosocial needs of the people we serve. As clinical social workers, we ought to understand that we play an important role by identifying the traumatic stress and emotional relationships when a person is diagnosed with mental illness, or a medical problem.

Guides for the Intervention with People with emotional Problems:

1. Be respectful.
2. Be calm. clear, and direct in the communication.
3. Be consistent and predictable.
4. Stablish limits, rules, and expectations.
5. Maintain professional distance.
6. Accept the client/patient as he/she is.
7. Attributing symptoms to the illness as personal.
8. Maintain a positive attitude even during failure.
9. Acknowledge and praise positive behavior.
10. Help the client/patient to make realistic goals and objectives.
11. Have the attitude of "I don't know" to difficult questions.

Bibliography

Abramson, J.S., Mizrahi, T. (1996). When Social Workers and Physicians Collaborate: Positive and negative interdisciplinary experiences. Journal of the National Association of Social Workers, 4, 2-28.

American Psychological Association (1979-1988). ¿What is Psychotherapy? In Bloch Sidney (Ed). An Introduction to the Psychotherapist. Oxford University Press, p. 92-92.

Bureau of US Census. American Fact Finder-Results. Factfinder.census.gov. Retrieved January 16-2020.

Bandura, A. (1997). Social Learning Theory. New York General Learning Press.

Betancourt, J. R. (2001). Cultural Competence. Marginal or Mainstream Movement? New England Journal of Medicine; 351: 953-955.

Campinha-Bacote, J. (1998). A Model and Instrument for Addressing Cultural Competence in Health Care. Journal of Nursing Education; 38 (5), 204-207. Google Scholar.

Carter, R. (Ed), (1999). Addressing Cultural Issues in Organizations. Beyond the Corporate Context. Thousand Oaks, CA: Sage Publications.

Guarnaccia, P. J. (2008). Panic attacks in the Latino population: Culturally bound and distinct from panic attacks?

Center for Clinical Social Work. (2007). What is the Difference Between Clinical and Non-Clinical Social Work? American Board of Examiners in Clinical Social Work.

Coon, D. (2001). Introduction to Psychology. Gateways to Mind and Behavior. Nineth edition. Warthworth.

Davidson, K. (1990). Role Blurring and the Social Worker's Search for a Clear Domain. Health and Social Work, 15, 228-234.

Desk Reference to the Diagnostic Criteria From DSM-5. American Psychiatric Association Publishing. Washington DC, London-England.

Diaz, Christina, J. J., Niño, Michael (2019). Familism and The Hispanic Health Advantage role of Immigrants Status. Sage Journals.

Dillon, F. R., De La Rosa, G. E., Ibáñez, J. (2013). Acculturative Stress and Diminishing Family Cohesion Among Latino Immigrants. Springer.

Engard, Brian. (2017). 5 Social Work Theories that inform practice. Social Work Helper.

Fernández, R. L., Das, amar, K., Weissman, César Alfonso Myrna. (2005-2011). Depression in US Hispanics: Diagnostic and Management Considerations in Family Practice. The Journal of The American Board of Family Practice, 18 (4), 282-296.

Garcés, C. M. (2002). The Social Worker in the Emergency Room. Doctoral Dissertation. Yeshiva University (WWSSW). New York.

Garcés, C. M. (2018). La Intervención del Trabajador Social en el Centro Hospitalario-Retos para la Profesión. Edición Revisada. Palibrio Publishing Company.

Garcés, C. M. (2019). Hospital Social Work Interventions. Gold Touch Publisher.

Giachello, A. (1999). Hispanic Health Rx. University of Chicago. Chicago Journal. Volume 98, Issue 5.

Green, J. (1999). Cultural Awareness in the Human Services. 3rd.ed. Englewood Cliffs, NJ. Prince Hall.

Gomez, A. Beloz, J. Altern, J. (2001). The Botánica as a Culturally Appropriate Health Care Option for Latinos.

Greshton, L. (2016). Clinical Social Work Practice and Reflection. An Overview.

Hispanics in the US. (2006). Census Bureau, Population Estimates.

Insel, T. R. ((2008). Assessing the Economic Cost of Serious Mental Illness. The American Journal of Psychiatry. 165 (6), 633-665.

Kim, D. (1999). Culturally Competence Practice. Pacific Grove, CA: Books/Cole.

Nathan Kline Institute Center of Excellence in Culturally Competent Mental Health. (2019). Evidenced Based Practices in Support of Cultural Competence in Mental Health Services.

Lewis, M. J., West, B., Bautista, L., Greenberg, A., Done-Pérez, I. (2005). Perceptions of Service Providers and community members on intimate partner violence within a Latino community. Health Education & Behavior. 32:69-83. (PubMed).

Lum, D. (1999). Cultural Competence Practice. Pacific Grove, CA: Books/Cole.

Navarro Vásquez, C. (2014). Pew Research Center Analysis of Decennial Census and American Community Survey (IPUMS).

National Association of Social Workers (2006). NASW Code of Ethics of The National Association of Social Workers. Washington DC: author.

National Association of Social Workers. (2012). NASW Clinical and Non-Clinical Social Work. Washington DC: Author.

National Association of Social Workers (2014). NASW History of Psychiatric Social Work. Washington DC: Author.

National Association of Social Workers (2016). NASW Standards for Social Work Practice in Health care Settings. Washington DC: Author.

National Institute of Mental Health (2009-2012). Mental Health. NAMI Latino Multicultural Action Center.

National Alliance on Mental Illness (2016).

Ortega, A. N., Rosenheck, R., Alegría, M. Desai, R. A. (2000). Acculturation and the Lifetime Risk of Psychiatric and Substance Use Disorder Among Hispanics. J. Nerv Ment Dis. 188 (11); 728-35. PubMed.

Pew Research Center (2014). Analysis of Decennial Census and American Community Survey (IPUMS).

Porto Pérez, J., Merino, M. (2017-2019). Definición de Curandero. (https://definicion.de.curandero/).

John Hopkins-Medicine (2019). Psychiatry and Behavioral Sciences: The History of Psychiatric Social Work.

The Hispanic Community in New York State (2016). Thomas, P., DiNapoli, New York state Comptroller. Nearly One in Five New Yorkers Identify as Hispanic or Latino.

Rogers, L-Sirin, P Rice, SR Sirin (2014). Acculturation and cultural mismatch and their influences on immigrant children and adolescents' wellbeing

Vega, W. A., López, S. R. (2001). Priority Issues in Latino Mental Health Services Research. Mental Health Research, Vol. 3, No. 4.

Diaz Christina, J. J., Niño, Michael. (2019). Familism and the Hispanic Health Advantage: The role of Immigrants status. Sage Journals.

Walker, S., Beckett, C. (2004-2005). Social Work Assessment and Intervention. Russel House Publishing Company.

World Health Organization (2014). Mental Health: A State of Wellbeing: Author.

www.ingramcontent.com/pod-product-compliance
Lightning Source LLC
Chambersburg PA
CBHW050012070726

47598CB00014B/735